> Much gratitude to all those who are saving lives on a daily. Thank you…the world needs you, because you are important and loved and very much appreciated. What would we do without you.

Fighting Demons: Giving Hope to Life

By

Dalelynn Gusman

Table of Contents

BIO: 1

INTRODUCTION: 2

Chapter 1 3

    FIGHTING DEMONS 3

Chapter 2 18

    LIFE 18

Chapter 3 22

    WORK 22

Chapter 4 24

    SOCIAL MEDIA 24

Chapter 5 28

    LOVE 28

Chapter 6 37

    FAMILY 37

BIO:

Dalelynn Gusman was born in 1984 in Hawaii and is the ninth of ten children. Her father was of Filipino descent and worked for the Board of Water Supply in Honolulu County in Hawaii for 34 years before he retired. Her mother was a native Hawaiian and a professional singer in a group called "Kaleo O Kalani," made popular through the years 1970s – 2000s. Ms. Gusman describes her mother as having a "natural gift" for singing and playing multiple instruments. The author credits her mother as a significant inspiration in her life and, specifically, for this book. "My mother followed her dreams," asserts Ms. Gusman, "and taught me to follow mine."

Hope Kam moved to Virginia from Hawaii in 2021. The influence of the Hawaiian culture is evident in Ms. Gusman hospitality to guests as she always offers food and is concerned for others' comfort. Furthermore, she keeps the temperature toasty in her apartment to mimic the tropical warmth of her native island.

This is Ms. Gusman first book. She is currently writing a second one that tells the experiences behind the inspirational wisdom in *Fighting Demons: Giving Hope to Life*.

Interviewed By: JADE GORMAN

Dalelynn Gusman

INTRODUCTION:

Hello reader…My name is Dalelynn. Thank you for supporting my journey.

Now before reading this book, I want you to take off your shoes, have a seat on the couch, and get comfortable while eating some of your favorite snacks.

This world is already whack, so here is my outlook on life. Please have an open mind when reading these short passages. I speak about love, life, and family.

These are conversations and experiences I've had with myself, with people in my reality, and with people online. They have tried to torment me in my mind, and this is how I spoke to them in real life. So read on.

These quotes stem from defending myself in the past. Having been physically and emotionally abused by people, places, and things that surround me.

Writing this book has been very meaningful to me because it reconnects me to the things that I hold so dear to my heart. I find that this is my deep-seated purpose in life, to help build what has been broken.

CHAPTER 1

FIGHTING DEMONS

Sometimes to move forward in life, I've got to take a few steps back and then slap myself in the face for doing that.

Getting into good vibes is never a bad thing.

Sometimes my tears are because I'm happy and excited; at the same time, I can't handle myself. Just bear with me, be patient. Ok.

Sometimes my tears make people want to die, but in reality, my heart was crushed into pieces and that turned into a big scar, as if someone beat it with a stick or lashed me with a knife.
My scars are invisible to the naked eye.
No one can see unless I speak them.

When I cannot connect to my roots and stay grounded, I lose focus on what's important to me.
When the roots are deep, you are immovable, and that can never be taken away from you because you are *"naturally connected"* to something greater and stronger in life.

I wasn't born to be liked,

I was born to stand out;

And be myself on purpose.

Know your limits or else they will blow up in your face.

Exploitation takes away the privacy of others.

When you exploit someone that knows nothing about you,

You're setting yourself up for a real big show. Expect it!

Human Rights!!!

If I am not being myself then something is wrong.

I don't change my character for the convenience of others.

And I don't have to step down to your level for you to see it.

I won't lower my standards because you are low, and that's not called arrogance.

I am not obligated to live my life on your terms.

Look for a public puppet elsewhere.

This is my life. Not yours.

And I am proud to say that my principles have never left me.

This one's for you class!

I am not your community service provider, so please look to the nearest pharmacy for your prescription.

I am not defined by a certain color or race or group of people.
If you want to get to know me, just ask.
There's no harm in asking.

When something is bothering me, I say it; otherwise, it'll keep repeating itself.
And that's a big NO, NO.
I was not created to let people walk all over me.

When you were raised royal and now entering a society of abnormality,
It becomes a culture shock.
My normal is not your normal
But exposure to differences is what brings understanding.

Stop comparing me to animals.
I am not an animal.
I am a human being.
There is a big difference…
We are not the same species.
Stop putting me in the middle of your shenanigans

If you're wondering where all this is coming from…just know, it's years of storing it.
Wait; the best is yet to come.

Just to clarify some things about me…

I am not vegan, but I do like to try different foods.

I don't drink alcohol, nor do I smoke, and I am straight as straight can be.

I hope this clears up things in your head about me. Much Love!

Women should take pride in themselves,

Have self-respect and dignity.

It's called self-control and integrity. Practice it daily.

Never again will I let anyone make me feel ashamed of being myself.

Trying to brainwash me as if being myself on purpose is a bad thing.

I will not step down to your level of thinking!!

I was not born to think like you.

So remember that!

Just because we are human doesn't mean we are all the same

In belief, in culture, in morals and experiences in life.

We are all different, but the majority of us are… the same.

We should have common sense to live a peaceful life which may be a mystery to other people.

Are we in a world of psychological dysfunction?
Because what you're doing is not helping.
So stop explaining the deep things of the mind.
We are not children here.
Why? Do we look like patients?
Idiots!!!

Sometimes the stories people make up in their minds need to be filtered out.
Because there's a whole other world outside of their minds that they haven't experienced yet.
And it's beautiful.
I don't know how else to say it.
But it goes hand in hand.

"He has made everything beautiful in its time. He has also set eternity in the human heart; yet no one can fathom what God has done from beginning to end." (Ecclesiastes 3:11)
The Lord makes things beautiful in due season.
Big change is coming…

Before you become a good leader, you must learn how to be a good follower.

When are people going to realize that nobody is harming them

Or is coming to harm them in anyway.

That only means you have social anxiety.

Sometimes people need to get a hold of themselves;

Because I get confused when someone is actually trying to talk to me.

And others are just making up convos in the background.

Please don't talk to me on a deep personal level.

Save your personal problems for Jesus, not me.

I don't have *"Problem Solver"* on my forehead.

Change the way you speak;

You change your whole thought process.

It's beautiful…

And it starts with gratitude and thankfulness daily.

Some people like to feed on your pain of grief and guilt

Because it makes them feel superior to you.

People are afraid of getting their feelings hurt;

But that's all part of life.

It builds character and strength.

People don't understand this but
What hurts you also hurts me
In all aspects of life.
We are no different in this sense.
Just remember that.

When you learn to let someone be; they will let you be also.
No worries. No stress.
Learn this and practice it daily.

"For sound advice is a beacon, good teaching is a light, moral discipline is a life path."
(Proverbs 6:23)
Learn what is good and you'll be content in life.

After the second session with your therapist, your therapist needed a therapist.
How else do I say it.

When a person has been through so much in life
Their perspective changes.
As if it was specifically designed in their favor.
Experience changes your perception of things.
So stop living in a bubble.

When you've lost everything in life

Integrity and dignity make a strong hold for you.

Resiliently building you back up from ashes to royalty.

Your past will never define who you are today.

So keep your sad stories to yourself because nobody's asking.

Suicide is not something to be proud of, nor is purposely hurting someone emotionally or physically for that matter,

These are not the answer.

For immediate help, call 911 and they will direct you to get proper help.

"Peace, I leave with you. My peace I give to you: not as the world gives do I give to you. Let not your heart be troubled, neither let it be afraid." (John 14:27)

When we get lost, the Lord will always guide us who seek to live a better life.

Just exercise your faith daily.

Stages of growth we women go through on a monthly.

Sometimes the pain is just normal for us and we can't tell the difference

Sometimes we are an emotional wreck.

And you just have to deal with it.

I am nobody's "Ho".

Did you look at yourself in the mirror?

You must be the "Ho".

If I'm "Man" then what are you? Half a human.

Make sure you can handle the energy you give out because I can make it come back 10 times stronger.

Why do people always think I have anxiety?
That's you, not me.
Stop laying your insecurities on me
As if I am exactly like you.
Bruh. We are different. Period!
Look for someone who thinks just like you
So both of you can have a short future together.

Loneliness is miserable, and they want me to be miserable too. "NO THANKS"
When people come around me with their attitude,
I can make their worst dreams come true.
Just wait your turn.

To those who think I'm toxic, thank you…that means you're miserable
And that makes me happy.
Good job! Narcissist.

Do not force your negativity or assumptions on me.
As a reminder take those things to Jesus
He is our Lord and Savior whom we can count on at any time
without even standing in line.
So learn how to pray and trust Him always. Okay!

Honestly…being misunderstood is not my problem "It's yours"
Good luck chuck.

He who teaches not to love oneself is teaching others to do the same.
Don't be the virus that spreads cancer, it will soon eat you up inside.
What are you *doing?*
Only few can understand this

When repetitive things keep showing up in your reality, it's time to put an end to those imaginations people keep of you in their mind.
I'm not living in your reality, I'm living in my reality.

If you have not walked a mile in my shoes or even an inch;
Then you have nothing to say to me.
Keep your negative comments to yourself.
I am not you and you are not me.

Know when to listen and know when to speak.
There's a time for everything.

Do not trash talk me.
That's how people get into fights and how wars are started.
So if you do that to me, this is what you're asking for.
Don't be that person.

Again…I do not play your silly games, nor do I compete with people
Simply because I can just be myself and no one can tell me otherwise.
Don't play survival games with me because you'll be the first one down.
Fricking kids.
And I'm talking about everyone in general
When are y'all gonna grow up?

Oh, I'm sorry, I forgot to bring the mirror
So you can talk to yourself.
Because nobody else is listening.

Critiquing every little thing someone does or says is called fear and insecurity.
Learn how to let it go; it'll just eat you up inside and you'll destroy yourself in the process.
No one else to blame but yourself.

Sometimes people don't know what is good because they've adapted themselves to what is bad.
And now that's all they know.
Someone needs to show them the light because they're lost.
This is serious guys. No jokes.

If something or someone makes you act out of character, then it's not for you.
Being your real self is a flex,
But it doesn't give you the right to be disrespectful and bitter.

Ain't this ironic?
Those who disrespected me are the ones teaching me how to be respectful?
Are you fudging kidding me?
Move niche, get out the way, get out the way, get out the way.
That doesn't fly with me, no way no.

When people are afraid of you,
They tend to make up stuff.
Just remember the truth is never afraid to be questioned.
So be real, don't fake, it's unnecessary.

Be in sync with what aligns for you, not what aligns for others.
Everyone is their own individual person
And in life there's always gonna be that gray area…
Only few can understand this.

It takes strength to say "NO" and actually do something about it.

I don't expect people to change;
People change on their own because they want to better themselves.
Now if you don't like my growth,
Best you step to the side so the world can be a better place
Without you.

People try to tell me how to live my life with less.
If you want to live with less everything, go back to Mars or Venus or wherever you came from.
Earth is not your home.

This is long overdue, but I do not tolerate people who tell me one thing and then do the opposite.
I am not one to sit down and wait for you until next year, next Christmas, next month, or next week.
Look at all the time that has been wasted and money spent doing nothing.

You're either gonna help me or step to the side so someone else,
Who is more deserving can do so.

Most of us humans don't need pity or sympathy,
We just need someone to help us get back on our feet.
Simple as that! People nowadays.

If you don't know what you're doing, just ask for help.
The risk is Not asking.

Convos become different when people open the eyes of their heart
instead of the ones they have in the back of their head.
When you come to realize this, your perspective changes…

I apologize if something went over my head or if I didn't get what
you were saying, but please be reassured if you approach me again, I
will be more than happy to speak to you.
Just pull me to the side or something;
That's the only way to get my attention; there's no harm in doing
that. Trust me.

Please don't get me mixed up with other people.
I don't have battles inside my head.
When I meet people in person, they fight themselves,
Not me.
And that's Facts!

If you don't know who is doing you wrong, or whatever the case may be, don't automictically assume it's a certain set of people or what have you.
Slow down your mind before you speak.

Stop exploiting people and forcing them into something they're not.
What's wrong with you?

People who cannot understand a certain phrase or concept take things to extreme measures where it is not necessary to do so.

I don't play your color games and my vision isn't black and white.
Go look for someone who is literally blind,
So both of you can end up in a ditch together with the same niche.

We are not living in the 1960s here,
Where the color of your skin separates you from the rest.
Grow Up! And be civil.

Sometimes I can relate to a certain generation more easily than others.
But that's just me.
I don't know about you.

CHAPTER 2

LIFE

When people don't like you, they teach you all kinds of irrelevant things that'll harm your body.
No wonder this world is whack.
Don't listen to those people.
It only means they don't like themselves and they want everyone to feel the same.

Teaching someone harmful things that are bad for their health and wellbeing
Will soon consume you.
It will eat you alive.
That's called reaping what you sowed.
Only a few can understand this

Don't ever be tempted to do alcohol, cigarettes or drugs.
Stay focused and remind yourself how far you've come without those toxic things.
Be thankful. Stay on track.

When the world finds out who's putting evil things in the minds of people,
Those MoFos will pay!

If you're going to invite someone out to have a cup of coffee or lunch (whatever it may be)
Don't make a fool of yourself when the check comes around the table.
Speaking from experience,
Never again.
But as for me, I do not bestow that on people.

Yesterday at the grocery store
Someone passed by me and said,
"Let's prepare the chicken wings."
And I was like
Ohh…Who's house?
Come on…be generous.
Don't keep it all to Yo Self.

Respect the food and stop wasting it,
Because there are others who are starving in this world and wanting what you have.
Be grateful for what you have
 A sense of thankfulness on a daily.
Life is more fulfilling that way.

If you can't eat the product(s) you sell in the stores, it was never yours to begin with.

They just added chemicals in there so they could say it was theirs from the start.

And then they say, "Oh, this is how it has always been."

You know who you are.

Stop doing that!

Inspections will be done and you better expect it.

Niche, fines and imprisonment will be yours....

When are we going to evaluate the health and quality of our food?

Inspections need to be done; limitations need to be placed.

It does more harm than good without these in place.

Solid foundations are built on God's blessings, With joy and clarity and peace.

Not confusion and chaos.

When people have malicious thoughts about you...they tend to repeat what you said in their mind instead of talking it out with you or talking to a friend about it.

A good friend. That is...you know.

One who'll give good advice.

Do you know what that means?

Or should I reiterate it to you?

Don't wear out visits with a friend.
You'll have none left.
Meaning…
Learn how to do things on your own
After they've taught you.
Don't always be dependent on them.
They have their own life too, Ya Know.

Shoutout to all my family and friends, you are incredible and an inspiration.
I love you all for guiding and supporting me throughout my mysterious journey.
You guys are the best!!
And I love it when you guys make me laugh.
I can't get those moments back, Thank you so much….

I have never lacked in showing gratitude to anyone that God has put in my life.
Forever thankful.
That part of me will never change for anything.

Much gratitude to all those who are saving lives on a daily. Thank you…the world needs you
Because you are important and loved and very much appreciated.
What would we do without you.

Chapter 3

WORK

The majority of society don't know anything about relationships and how to respect one another.
It's as if I'm teaching big kids here.
What are you showing the younger generation?

I'm done with people trying to bribe me.
Niche, keep them dirty monies to yourself.

I don't keep up with numbers,
the numbers keep up with me.

I don't like people wasting my time nor money.
Everybody wants to get paid, but nobody wants to work.
If you're stalling time just because…don't expect work to be waiting for you the next time around.
You have just lost your job.

If you haven't worked a day in your life to receive what you got today,
Don't strut around town as if you did.
It's good to be grateful always on a daily.

What breaks my heart the most is when I want to volunteer,
But there's no place for me.

CHAPTER 4

SOCIAL MEDIA

To all those who like to analyze my page after every post or what have you,
And say toxic things to me. Go love yourself.
This one's for you. Have a good morning.

Your social media account is like a house.
Be careful who you invite in.
Not everyone is who they say they are, and pretty pictures are sometimes deceiving.
Be aware. Don't dare.

Posting things on my page keeps me on track and helps me to stay disciplined.
It's always good to look back at your content and adjust if needed.
Hope this helps anyone else out there.

The less violence and trash talk people do on social media or any media platform,
The better things will be and mental health issues will no longer exist.
Mental health in plain sight. Hello…peoples….
You're on it every day!

TBH guys, we're literally laughing at you because ya'll don't like each other.
IDK why tho...
But I think it's super funny.

Most don't even have history,
So they won't know what you're talking about.
You don't know what you're doing.
People know how to think for themselves
So stop teaching them how to think.

People are not obligated to open up and speak about their past
Because the majority of this society are just plain "Nosy."
They use your past against you and torture you in every and any kind of way they can.
Just so they can bring you down with them.
This is the level of embarrassment society has on us humans and dozens more that are on the internet.

For all those who like to hack onto people's things and LIVE THERE.
Don't be surprised if you get evicted. BY FORCE!
All bad things come to an end.

If people don't bring anything to your table, cut them off.
Let them scramble for themselves.
Clean your feed out daily until all the trash is gone or close your account for peace of mind.
Don't be afraid to lose those memories
because you can always make new ones.

Search engines don't like me because I'm the most feared in all the universe.
Tough niche right here.

I am not a perfectionist but if that's how you see me, then it is my honor to be your inspiration.
Sometimes people learn by living as an example.

Seriously. People need to stop following me with their fake accounts and… posting fake content.
People be too obsessed here.
Get over it!!

Yall can keep Your competitive attitude to yourself.
And leave me out of it.
Not my problem if you see me as a competition "Unfriend Me."

I don't make idols of people's feelings,
And if I tell you about me and the things I like, and you don't like it,
Then "Unfriend Me." I'm not for everyone.

I don't know about you but when people get ghosted, it's normally not by a true human.
Sorry to say.
Speaking from numerous experiences.
And I am not a runner, it's people who run away from me.
Not my fault they get nervous around me.

Some people like to wear their story on the outside,
But I wear mine on the inside.

I personally don't like "Tatts",
Is it a trend?
Or a….
"You belong to me" kind of thing?
I don't get it.
Because I would never put someone's name or pix
Or anything else on my body for that reason,
Or any reason at all…To be frank.

CHAPTER 5

LOVE

These are some of my thoughts on Love:
Humans know how to love humans,
But I can't define love for others
Because they need to find it themselves.
We don't live in our imagination,
We make it our reality.
That is our freedom of choice.

Whoever said that you have to suffer in life?
Suffering means pain.
Is that how you love? Or
Is that how you want to be loved?

Ladies or guys, don't enter a relationship if your heart has not healed yet from the previous.
It wouldn't be fair for the next person.
Be true to yourself and to others,
If you're unsure,
Just say you're not ready.
Simple as that.

You want a relationship with "No Label"
Leaving the other person questioning themselves...

Then why you so obsessed with me?
Be real!
"What are we?"
Stop giving mixed signals here.

Relationship advice:
Don't force someone to love you, even though you might love them.
It will not turn out well in the end.
The heart is not something to be meddled with.

No one should be required to be in a relationship for any reason,
99% of the time, it won't work out.
Relationships don't work out because people have the wrong mentality.

Don't expect me to read your mind.
Speak to me or forever hold your peace.

When are you going to stop playing these silly games where men vs. women and vice versa.
Leave those silly games at home.
Don't bring it in public.
Silly people, silly games, begets a stupid system.

Women should never put down men, especially when they are trying to express how they feel. Men need respect, love, and understanding also, not just women.

What are women doing these days?

To all the men out there…

When you look for a woman, make sure she's "Beautiful on the inside," not just the outside.

Don't be blinded by looks alone,

Open your eyes and listen to your heart.

Why do people fall in love so easily?

Just for the feeling of being infatuated by it?

Or do they just get offended when the content isn't about them?

Signs you have not matured yet:

You are easily offended by others,

You don't know how to communicate your feelings or emotions clearly.

Nor do you know how to apologize when you are wrong

And you don't take the time to correct your bad habits.

If you like someone, have the courage to tell them;

If not, then you're probably afraid of rejection.

Sorry to say…

But unashamed and confident people don't have this problem.

If you cannot appreciate yourself for how you were created, then you cannot appreciate others.
And to have a love in your life; it'll be too self-sacrificing because of you.
Don't ever let someone carry your insecurities. Grow Up!!

Don't meddle with people's love life, your future will be ruined,
Just as much as you ruined theirs.
This is "Human Rights."

People be talking about having a good woman or a good man, but the conversation keeps going around in circles.
I have a headache.
Sounds like a broken record, so annoying.

How can you possibly know what the standards are in a relationship,
When you can't even give them to yourself.
People expecting high standards? Please…. you need to get over yourself.

I don't want relationship advice.
If you don't know how to treat a woman, then go find someone who will treat you exactly how you treat yourself,
Because that's the standard you set.

Don't try to be perfect for your partner.

No one is perfect.

Perfection is only in the mind, but if you want that,

Then work on yourself first.

Perfection is actually a broad spectrum.

It's only you who define that on your own;

Then, your heart will follow and lead you to the right person.

Now here we go…

For those women out there…

If your man works hard,

Provides for you,

Respects you as much as they respect themselves,

He's a keeper.

Don't ever let him go.

These are must haves, girl…

Communication is Key

Everywhere you go.

But once you lose that in a relationship;

It's hard to patch.

And unfortunately, this can go on for years…

Unknowingly and unaware.

The one who stays consistent
In a relationship
Is the stronger one.
Now if both are consistent,
They make for a good team,
And love is what binds them together.

If someone sees you as a competition, that means they don't like you.
And they just wanna play with your feelings.

My life isn't a competition and never was.
People are always fighting to have me in theirs,
But this time….
I choose myself
Before I choose you.
Ain't no competition here.
The only person I compete with is myself.

Being corky and cheesy is cute, and if you don't like it,
It's not my problem….

When you have two genuine people who truly love each other.
Know when to stop your silly games, please, because it will backfire in your face.

I don't know how to play your silly games,

So don't expect me to play with your trashy feelings.

You can have them or just give them to someone else,

So both of you can go downhill to lonely Ville.

I wear what I want to wear, so don't try to run games on me because it won't work.

Like I said before;

Keep your games to yourself!

You won't like what I say, especially when I have myself on repeat.

Stop treating me like a game…

Because you'll be the first one to lose.

I said what I said, and I mean what I say.

I don't have time for your nonsense,

Myself is waiting for me on the other side.

Now here's a kicker….

Sometimes if you and your partner don't have the same morals or values in life,

Then your relationship won't last long,

Something to think about.

When a guy says: "Let's have seggs in my parents' bedroom" and the girl refuses to do so.
You know she was raised well.
And I am not like this society that lives without morals.
We are not the same.

When you're sick of all the ex's that treated you like trash.
This comeback is very personal,
And it's all about me.
Just wait and see…
Repetitive cycle breaker.
Damn…something NEW IS KEY.
Changes everything, girl.

My mom taught me this about relationships:
Never tattoo your partner's name or picture on your body.
Because they are not obligated to stay in your life,
And you can't hold their feelings for you.
It's freely given not forced.
Lessons to learn people…

If you break up with your partner,
Make sure you don't date within his or her circle
Because you will be the talk of the town.
How embarrassing…

Your house is a reflection of who you are
May, you always keep it clean.

Chapter 6

FAMILY

When you have your own family, the feeling is bliss.
Family helps you to relearn yourself throughout your journey.
Feel it, live it, be blessed in it.

Those who know the meaning of family, know how to treat their partner.
But to take the life of your partner is never an option to carry.
Get that mentality out your mind.
What is wrong with you?
Death is not a company of life.

Love is not just an emotion but is shown…through actual deeds.
Consistent and long suffering, it never fades…
Definitely a beautiful trait one can possess.
Something lived but never told.
Beautiful things are hidden so well, people are looking for it,
they're yearning for it,
and wanting it,
Because not everybody has it,
Like a missing piece to a puzzle.
And the one who has it, is normally the one blind to it.
Thinking they're not enough.

The Lord's blessing doesn't come with pain,

it comes with discipline and joy;

Enough for you to share with others.

Young people…

If you want to be successful in life, do these five things daily

1) Clean the house
2) Wash your clothes
3) Take care of your personal hygiene
4) Exercise
5) Manage your money well

Then the rest will follow…

Once you have these five steps down, it'll be a piece of cake.

I don't blame parents if they teach their children to pick from their own garden,

Because they know that the food quality in our country has gone downhill.

When are we going to live up to the standards we've set before?

We pride ourselves on these high standards of living.

This is one of the reasons why we are envied by many nations…

It needs to be bought back to reality.

It's totally normal to feel the need for someone to be by your side when you're lonely.
But that's what family is for so that you'll never feel that way.
They're always there for you no matter what.
I have a family that regards my happiness and that, is enough.

My Toxic trait:
Being raised with more brothers than sisters.
Nothing can compare to possessing the same traits as my siblings.
I love them just as much as they love me,
And no one makes them cry, except me.

I don't tolerate people who do not respect their family.
Only shows how much they respect themselves as well as others.
For those who grew up in a close-knit family like me, it means everything.

People who break up happy families are the most miserable
Because they don't have a family of their own.
Manic loners.
Mental Health peoples…
They always want to destroy the happiness of others due to unexplained jealousy or hatred.

Children learn by example, so be a good example to them.

Now I see why my parents were super strict with me when I was growing up.

So, I don't end up like the rest of society who practice lawlessness.

I am not like you

Don't get me mixed up

We are not the same.

In this younger generation, they have guidance issues.

Parents are not really parents and so children seek advice from peers.

Can you blame them? For seeking what is good?

Topic worth exploring….

Why do people have to exaggerate good things in life?

And make it seem like it's bad.

Don't you know you're scaring the younger generations…as if it's something deadly to expect.

When it's not.

This is the onset of anxiety and depression when nothing has happened yet.

Imaginations only…. Hello….

In a world where children feel their parents don't care for them,
Is a world full of sorrow and no guidance.
Without moral and emotional support towards our younger generations,
You only repeat the past daily and nothing changes.
GIVE THEM A BRIGHTER FUTURE!!

When parents have problems, the children can feel it.
Relationships are not a competition, it's about finding common ground,
And sometimes it's about learning to let go because nothing's working.
Time spent apart can heal a broken heart.
It's called reflecting…

It's hard when you've been raising everyone else's kids but your own.
Because your real kids get the stressed end of you not the real affectionate attention they actually need.

Respect the women that are pregnant.
They're carrying our future.

www.ingramcontent.com/pod-product-compliance
Lightning Source LLC
Chambersburg PA
CBHW070749050426
42449CB00010B/2399